גְּבוּרוֹת

If you've ever seen a lightning storm, you've witnessed God's power in nature. And if you've watched the first leaves bloom on your favorite backyard tree after a long, cold winter, you've observed God's power to give and sustain life.

The second blessing of the Amidah is called גְּבוּרוֹת ("powers"). In it, we praise God's awesome powers. These powers are evidence of God's greatness—the same greatness that gives us life and the strength to make the world a better place.

Practice reading the גְּבוּרוֹת aloud.

1. אַתָּה גִבּוֹר לְעוֹלָם, אֲדֹנָי, מְחַיֶּה הַכֹּל/מֵתִים אַתָּה, רַב לְהוֹשִׁיעַ.

2. מְכַלְכֵּל חַיִּים בְּחֶסֶד, מְחַיֶּה הַכֹּל/מֵתִים בְּרַחֲמִים רַבִּים. סוֹמֵךְ

3. נוֹפְלִים, וְרוֹפֵא חוֹלִים, וּמַתִּיר אֲסוּרִים, וּמְקַיֵּם אֱמוּנָתוֹ לִישֵׁנֵי עָפָר.

4. מִי כָמוֹךָ, בַּעַל גְּבוּרוֹת, וּמִי דוֹמֶה לָּךְ, מֶלֶךְ מֵמִית וּמְחַיֶּה

5. וּמַצְמִיחַ יְשׁוּעָה?

6. וְנֶאֱמָן אַתָּה לְהַחֲיוֹת הַכֹּל/מֵתִים. בָּרוּךְ אַתָּה, יְיָ,

7. מְחַיֶּה הַכֹּל/הַמֵּתִים.

You are eternally mighty (powerful), Adonai, You give life to all/the dead, great is Your power to save.

With kindness You sustain the living, with great compassion (mercy) give life to all/the dead. You help the falling, and heal the sick, and You free the captive, and keep faith with those who sleep in the dust.

Who is like You, God of Power, and who is comparable to You, Ruler who brings death and gives life and who is a source of salvation?

You are faithful to give life to all/the dead. Blessed are You, Adonai, who gives life to all/the dead.

Prayer Dictionary

אַתָּה
you (are)

גִּבּוֹר
mighty, powerful

לְעוֹלָם
eternally

מְחַיֶּה
give life

לְהוֹשִׁיעַ
to save

חַיִּים
life, the living

בְּרַחֲמִים
with compassion, mercy

מִי כָמוֹךָ
who is like you?

WHAT'S MISSING?

Fill in the missing word(s) in each Hebrew phrase.

1. אַתָּה _____ לְעוֹלָם, אֲדֹנָי

You are eternally *mighty (powerful)*, Adonai

2. רַב _____

great is your power *to save*

3. מְכַלְכֵּל _____ בְּחֶסֶד

with kindness you sustain *life (the living)*

4. _____ , בַּעַל גְּבוּרוֹת

who is like you, God of Power

PRAYER VARIATIONS

Reform and Reconstructionist prayer books use the phrase
מְחַיֶּה כֹּל חַי and מְחַיֶּה הַכֹּל ("gives life to everything") in
the גְבוּרוֹת. Conservative and Orthodox prayer books contain
the words מְחַיֶּה הַמֵּתִים ("revives the dead").

The concept of "reviving the dead" is called *resurrection*.
Belief in resurrection is the belief that, at some time in the
future, all those who have died will be brought back to life
by God.

Some people interpret the phrase "reviving the dead"
symbolically, and use it to refer to the cycle of nature. For
example, plants that are dormant and animals that hibernate
in the winter become active again in the spring.

Whether or not they believe in resurrection, most Jews
believe that the soul (נֶפֶשׁ) lives on forever. The soul is a part
of God in each of us.

Which version of the גְבוּרוֹת is found in your synagogue's
prayer book?

POWERFUL WORDS

Circle the Hebrew word or phrase that means the same as the English.

who is like you?	מִי כָמוֹךָ	חֲסָדִים טוֹבִים	לְעוֹלָם וָעֶד
life, the living	אֱמֶת	זִכָּרוֹן	חַיִּים
eternally	עֶלְיוֹן	לְעוֹלָם	וָעַל
mighty, powerful	גִּבּוֹר	גּוֹמֵל	מֶלֶךְ
you (are)	אֶחָד	אַתָּה	אָבוֹת
give life	מְחַיֶּה	מָגֵן	מוֹשִׁיעַ
with compassion, mercy	וּבְרָצוֹן	בְּרַחֲמִים	בְּאַהֲבָה
to save	לְהוֹשִׁיעַ	לִיצִיאַת	לְהַדְלִיק

IT'S A MATCH!

Match the Hebrew word to its English meaning.

give life	גִּבּוֹר
life, the living	מְחַיֶּה
eternally	חַיִּים
mighty, powerful	לְעוֹלָם

3

THEME OF גְּבוּרוֹת

The גְּבוּרוֹת praises God's power, or ability, to:

1. create life
2. save life
3. sustain life

4. help the falling
5. heal the sick
6. free the captive

Since we are created in God's image (בְּצֶלֶם אֱלֹהִים), we have the ability to act in godly ways.

Choose 3 of God's powers from the list above, and give an example of what people can do to imitate God. Here is one example:

heal the sick—We can become doctors or nurses who work to cure illness and disease.

1. _____

2. _____

3. _____

Holding a baby can fill us with the wonder of God's creations and all the possibilities that the future can bring.

4

WHERE ARE WE?

Let's put the גְבוּרוֹת in the context of a prayer service.

Every prayer service contains a version of the עֲמִידָה.
The first three and the last three blessings of every
עֲמִידָה are blessings of praise and are always the same.
Only the middle בְּרָכוֹת change.

גְבוּרוֹת is the *second* blessing in the עֲמִידָה.

What is the name of the *first* blessing in the עֲמִידָה?
Write your answer in Hebrew and in English.

Hebrew: _____

English: _____

Do you recall the theme or subject of the first blessing in the עֲמִידָה? Write it here.

_____

אָבוֹת
▶ גְבוּרוֹת
קְדוּשָׁה
קְדוּשַׁת הַיּוֹם
עֲבוֹדָה
הוֹדָאָה
בִּרְכַּת שָׁלוֹם

We feel God's presence in the world through acts of kindness and compassion.
The Jewish communities of France donated this ambulance to the State of Israel
to help heal the sick and save lives.

Prayer Building Blocks

אַתָּה גִבּוֹר לְעוֹלָם "you are eternally mighty (powerful)"

אַתָּה means "you."

Whom are we addressing? _____

גִבּוֹר means "mighty" or "powerful."

Write the name of the blessing you are studying. _____

Can you see the connection between the word גִבּוֹר and the name of the blessing?

Both words mean _____.

לְעוֹלָם means "eternally" or "forever."

לְעוֹלָם וָעֶד also means "eternally" or "forever."

Draw a circle around the words לְעוֹלָם וָעֶד or לְעוֹלָם wherever they appear below.

Practice reading the sentences aloud.

1. וְלֹא נֵבוֹשׁ לְעוֹלָם וָעֶד.

2. בָּרוּךְ יְיָ הַמְבֹרָךְ לְעוֹלָם וָעֶד.

3. דָּבָר טוֹב וְקַיָּם לְעוֹלָם וָעֶד.

4. שָׁלוֹם רָב עַל־יִשְׂרָאֵל עַמְּךָ תָּשִׂים לְעֹלָם.

5. בֵּינִי וּבֵין בְּנֵי יִשְׂרָאֵל אוֹת הִיא לְעוֹלָם.

6. אֵל חַי וְקַיָּם, תָּמִיד יִמְלֹךְ עָלֵינוּ לְעוֹלָם וָעֶד.

6

מְחַיֶּה "give life"

מְחַיֶּה means "give life."

The root of מְחַיֶּה is חיה.

The root חיה tells us that "life" is part of a word's meaning.

In each sentence below circle the word(s) with the root חיה.

(Remember: Sometimes a root letter is missing from a word.)

Practice reading the sentences aloud.

1. עַם יִשְׂרָאֵל חַי. עוֹד אָבִינוּ חַי.

2. כִּי הֵם חַיֵּינוּ וְאֹרֶךְ יָמֵינוּ.

3. בָּרוּךְ אַתָּה, יְיָ אֱלֹהֵינוּ, מֶלֶךְ הָעוֹלָם, אֲשֶׁר נָתַן-לָנוּ
   תּוֹרַת אֱמֶת וְחַיֵּי עוֹלָם נָטַע בְּתוֹכֵנוּ.

4. דָּוִד מֶלֶךְ יִשְׂרָאֵל חַי וְקַיָּם.

5. וְתִתֶּן לָנוּ חַיִּים אֲרֻכִּים, חַיִּים שֶׁל שָׁלוֹם, חַיִּים שֶׁל
   טוֹבָה, חַיִּים שֶׁל בְּרָכָה.

6. וְיַמְלִיךְ מַלְכוּתֵהּ בְּחַיֵּיכוֹן וּבְיוֹמֵיכוֹן וּבְחַיֵּי דְכָל-בֵּית יִשְׂרָאֵל.

Look back at the גְבוּרוֹת blessing on page 16. Circle all the words with
the root חיה. How many words did you circle? _____

מְכַלְכֵּל חַיִּים בְּחֶסֶד "with kindness you sustain the living"

חַיִּים means "living" or "life."

Write the root of חַיִּים. _____ _____ _____

בְּחֶסֶד means "with kindness."

בְּ means _____.

חֶסֶד means _____.

"LIVELY" TIDBITS

- Did you ever see grownups clink glasses and toast each other with the word "לְחַיִּים"—"To Life!"?

- Is there someone in your class wearing a חַי necklace? We know that חַי means "life."

- Did you know that each Hebrew letter also has a numerical value? There's even a system—called *gematria*—of interpreting a Hebrew word by adding up the value of its letters. For example, the letter ח has the value 8 and the letter י has the value 10. Together they add up to 18—and they spell the word חַי! That's why we often give monetary gifts at Jewish celebrations in multiples of $18.

  Why do you think it is appropriate to give gifts in multiples of $18?

  _____

  _____

People often give gifts in multiples of $18 in celebration of weddings and other lifecycle events.

בְּרַחֲמִים רַבִּים "with great compassion"

בְּרַחֲמִים means "with compassion" or "with mercy."

בְּ means _____.

רַחֲמִים means _____.

The root of בְּרַחֲמִים is רחמ.

The root רחמ tells us that "compassion" or "mercy" is part of a word's meaning.

God is sometimes referred to as אֵל מָלֵא רַחֲמִים.

Fill in the missing word in the English translation of that phrase.

God full of _____.

Here are three other names by which God is known. Circle the root letters רחמ in each phrase.

אַב הָרַחֲמִים
Merciful Parent

אֵל חַנּוּן וְרַחוּם
Gracious and Compassionate God

הָרַחֲמָן
The Merciful One

The Talmud tells us that if we expect compassion from God, we should show compassion to others. Describe one way you can show compassion to others.

_____

_____

מִי כָמוֹךָ "who is like you?"

מִי כָמוֹךָ means "who is like you."

מִי means _____ .

כָמוֹךָ means _____ .

כָמוֹ means "like."

ךָ at the end of a word means _____ .

Circle כָמוֹךָ or כָמְכָה in each line below. Then read each line.

1. אֵין כָמוֹךָ בָאֱלֹהִים, אֲדֹנָי, וְאֵין כְמַעֲשֶׂיךָ.

2. מִי־כָמֹכָה בָאֵלִם, יְיָ?

3. מִי כָמֹכָה, נֶאְדָר בַּקֹדֶשׁ.

CHALLENGE QUESTION:

Do you remember the prayer that begins on line 2 above? When did the children of Israel first sing these words?

_____

_____

An Ethical Echo

Just as our tradition teaches that God heals the sick (רוֹפֵא חוֹלִים),
so also we can help a sick person feel better. For example, we can visit,
a mitzvah known as בִקוּר חוֹלִים. Sharing time with someone who is
ill can put that person in a happier mood. While doctors can help cure
someone physically, the Bible teaches us—and modern science shows—
that lifting the spirits of the ill can ease and speed their recovery.

Think About This!

Maybe the last time you were sick your best friend stopped by
to tell you a joke, or your little sister made you a cute drawing.
What else can you do to brighten the day of someone who is
feeling poorly? What should you avoid doing or saying?

WHO'S YOUR HERO?

The word גִּבּוֹר means "mighty," "powerful," or "hero." A hero is somebody who does something brave, like climbing Mt. Everest, or who helps make the world a better place, like a doctor who discovers the cure for a disease. You too can be a hero by doing something brave or by helping others.

1. Name a hero from Jewish history who acted bravely *and* helped the Jewish people. Describe what he or she did.

    _____

    _____

    _____

2. Describe something brave that *you* have done. Did it help to make your home, school, or even the world a better place? Explain your answer.

    _____

    _____

    _____

A hero isn't just someone who climbs mountains or saves lives. For example, Israeli scouts such as these are heroes when they help feed those in need.

Some congregations include בִּרְכַּת כֹּהֲנִים ("the Priestly Blessing") as part of the Amidah. These words were recited by the כֹּהֲנִים (priests) who served in the ancient Temple about 2,000 years ago. The prayer asks God to bless us, to be gracious to us, and to give us peace.

Practice reading בִּרְכַּת כֹּהֲנִים below.

1. יְבָרֶכְךָ יְיָ וְיִשְׁמְרֶךָ.

2. יָאֵר יְיָ פָּנָיו אֵלֶיךָ וִיחֻנֶּךָּ.

3. יִשָּׂא יְיָ פָּנָיו אֵלֶיךָ וְיָשֵׂם לְךָ שָׁלוֹם.

May God bless you and keep you.
May God's face shine upon you and be gracious to you.
May God's face be lifted to you and may God grant you peace.

Some parents bless their children with these words on Friday evenings when they are together at the Shabbat dinner table. Why do you think it is especially appropriate for parents to say these words to their children?

_____

_____